First published in 2025 by Hornblower Press
4 St. John's Crescent
Bishop Monkton HG3 3QZ
www.hornblowerpress.wordpress.com

All poems copyright © the individual poets

All rights reserved. No part of this publication may be reproduced, stored in a retrieval system, or transmitted in any form or by any means (electronic, mechanical, photocopying, recording, or otherwise), without the prior written permission of the publisher.

ISBN 978-1-0687315-0-1

Cover photo: Leah Fletcher
Formatting and Cover Art: DAZED Designs

This Here This Now

Anthology of Ripon Poets 2025

edited by
Leah Fletcher & Caroline Matusiak

HORNBLOWER
PRESS

Contents

Introduction   ix

The Poems

RIPON'S HEARTBEAT   3
Gemma Johnson

ELEGY WRITTEN IN RIPON MARKET PLACE   4
Maggie Cobbett

RIPON MARKET DAY   5
Sue Birch

THE BELLS   6
Hazel Christelow

RIPON CATHEDRAL BELLS   7
Geoffrey W. Johnson

NUMBERS   8
Felicity Hydes

NOBLESSE OBLIGE   10
Maggie Cobbett

TIN SOLDIER   12
Kate Swann

RIPON   13
Timmy Anglais

BUS TO RIPON   14
Caroline Matusiak

GOING DOWNHILL ON A BICYCLE   15
Susan Perkins

MALCOM DIXON MAN OF RIPON   16
Terence Neal

BENEATH THE BANDSTAND   17
Nicky Hasson

THE RIPON COLLEGE INTERVIEW   18
Lesley Davy

CORRIDORS OF LEARNING Eileen Thompson	19
NORTH BRIDGE Carol Burdett Mayer	21
FISHING ON THE URE Kate Swann	22
IT HAS TO LEAD TO THE SEA Peter J Donnelly	23
THE LIMITS Felicity Hydes	24
THE LAVER Peter J Donnelly	25
BIRDS OF THE WETLANDS Susanna Lewis	26
THE NATURE RESERVE IN WINTER Sheila Whitfield	27
YET ANOTHER AUTUMN POEM Sheila Whitfield	28
ST JOHN'S, SHAROW Caroline Matusiak	29
BISHOPTON WOODS Leila Roberts	30
TURNING LEAVES Gemma Johnson	31
GHOSTS OF FOUNTAINS ABBEY Susanna Lewis	32
GREWELTHORPE GRAVEDIGGERS Tim Harrison	33
DUSK WALK Ian Clarke	34
FELLING LARCHES Tim Harrison	35
STAVELEY STARLINGS Helen Watkinson	37
THE THORNBOROUGH HENGES Paul Mills	38

NIDDERDALE Sue Birch	39
THE HANDKERCHIEF TREE Claire Shackleton	41
SWIMMING AT COFFIN LAKE Charlotte Wilson	42
REVERIE WRITTEN IN A COUNTRY CHURCHYARD Marilyn Longstaff	44
HEARTSCAPE Claire Shackleton	46
THE SWING AT HEPTONSTALL Paul Mills	48
WHITE BIRD Peter Bell	49
SALIENT Philippa Graham	50
THE COSMONAUTS OF ULM Andy Croft	52
MOLYVOS Andy Croft	53
MID-ATLANTIC Leah Fletcher	54
DEFORESTATION Molly Hall	55
THE PLATES Peter J Page	56
THE MOVEMENT OF THE PEOPLE Helen Watkinson	57
THE WISHING STONE John Ridley	58
SCHOOL PHOTOGRAPH (1957) John Ridley	59
THE BOY FROM MY SCHOOL YEAR WHO'S DOING BETTER THAN EVERYONE ELSE Nick Edwards	60

THE WAITING TREE 61
Molly Hall

OR SO YOU SAID ONE DAY 62
Alexandre Mexis

MY TIME IS WORTH LESS NOW 64
Sadie Hasson

MUM'S ROAST 65
Leah Fletcher

LA MOUETTE 66
Philippa Graham

HEAD SPACE 68
Nicky Hasson

CRYSTAL MORNING 70
Linda Birkinshaw

THE END OF THE AFFAIR 71
Marilyn Longstaff

WHEN I AM DEAD 72
Duncan Thompson

BOREDOM 73
Nick Edwards

THE WAITING-ROOM MIRROR 74
Peter Burgham

FOR REAL 75
Alexandre Mexis

MAY 76
Leila Roberts

PONDLIFE 77
Charlotte Wilson

SOMETIMES I DON'T EVEN NOTICE 78
Ben Stanbridge

TREKKING 79
Peter Burgham

The Poets

The Poets 83

Introduction

Cross the market square in Ripon to find a poet. Perhaps, the barista serving coffee or the care worker returning from a late shift. Poetry sounds in the footsteps. From bars and cafes, the scribble of a pencil or the tap of a screen precede deliberation and consultation as writing groups meet over a cup of coffee or something stronger. Their contributions can be found in this book.

Two giants tower over the popularity of poetry here: Ripon College, now closed, but its legacy lives on, and the Ripon Poetry Festival. The festival was founded in 2016 by local poets, David McAndrew, Elizabeth Spearman, Paul Mills and Andy Croft.

It is a privilege to include the poems of tutors and students of the former Ripon College. Exuding from the biographies is a place of fond memories and nurtured talents.

The Ripon Poetry Festival nourishes grassroots poetry. Its mission to showcase emerging writers has given confidence and a stage to many, including myself. It also attracts established poets who choose to launch their books there.

Folk are writing on a bus as it jolts along, walking the dog while speaking phrases into a phone and at home at the kitchen table inspired by the tranquility of local landscape, the colourful clatter of market day or the challenge of daily life. Take a look at the biographies. They display a bunting of local people.

If poetry is life. Life lived. Then here is life lived in Ripon, in the words of our poets.

— *Caroline Matusiak*

The Poems

Ripon's Heartbeat

Gemma Johnson

In Ripon's embrace, where rivers sigh,
Cathedral spires pierce Yorkshire sky.
Ancient walls murmur tales of grace;
The market square holds time in place.
The hornblower calls with evening's light,
Through cobbled lanes that fade from night.
Studley's groves, where fountains gleam,
Deer step softly, as in a dream.
The abbey's bones guard secrets deep
Of monks who prayed where shadows sleep.
Ripon whispers through woodland shade,
A hymn of roots and history made.
Sunsets blaze in amber hues;
Fields grow still as evening dews.
The city's story etched in stone,
A timeless tale forever known.

Elegy Written in Ripon Market Place

with apologies to Thomas Gray

Maggie Cobbett

Four horn blasts toll the knell of parting day.
The tourists leave. There's nothing else to see.
Late shoppers homeward plod their weary way
And leave the square to squalor and to me.

Now shine the streetlights on the sight
Of stubbed out cigarettes, so dearly bought
By smokers who think they have the right
To miss the bins but never go to court.

Gum chewers too are careless in their aim
And dog owners ignore the public's moans.
Street drinkers too must take their share of blame
For broken glass upon the new laid stones.

The gluttons, worst of all, have passed this way.
Discarded wrappings prove they've had their share
Of pizza, kebabs, fish and chips, yet may
Still have found room for more gut-busting fare.

For many a box of polystyrene
A greasy take-home portion bear
And many a binger, growing green,
Adds their aroma to the Ripon air.

Ripon Market Day

Sue Birch

Come to Ripon! Come this way!
Bring your friends – it's Market Day!
Thursday or Saturday, starting early
Vibrant, colourful, hurly-burly
Bread and cakes, cheese and eggs
The freshest of local fruit and veg
Choice cuts of meat and gleaming fish
To make a truly mouth-watering dish
A beautiful setting in the market square
The historic obelisk standing there
The grand Town Hall, to the south, stands proud
Pubs and charity shops draw the crowd
Shoes for all seasons, books and mags
A rainbow of colours of clothes and bags
Or pretty material to make your own
Plants for the garden, dog bed or bone
Mouth-watering nibbles for a special treat
Garden furniture, picture frames and sweets
Schoolchildren selling home-made goodies
With their teachers and classroom buddies
A myriad of cafes offering a tempting lunch
Coffee & cake, just a cuppa or brunch
With many more outlets to tempt the punter
Whether high end shopper or bargain hunter
Take a window seat and soak in the action
Ripon's marketplace is quite an attraction
Enjoy the sights, the sounds and smells
And all within earshot of the cathedral bells

The Bells

Hazel Christelow

Before one thousand years were up
Anchored fast on jutting rock
Ripon Cathedral stood square and squat
Stones of Wilfrid, traveller, saint,
Out of Rome pilgrimage hard
Sowing the ripened Gospel Word
As seed upon a fallow field.
Bells of bronze, their mighty song
Forged in the foundry, the message tell,
Morning, evening timely chiming
Cataracts of tumbling sound,
Sally ropes with eight-fold peal,
Ringing changes, mathematical, precise,
Grandsire, steadman gathering pace.
Answer their bidding when they call,
As down the ages multitudes
From hill and dale have come and heard
And with the bells have sung aloud
Sweet resounding hymns of praise.

Ripon Cathedral Bells

Geoffrey W. Johnson

Climbing the spiral staircase,
The ropes hanging in a circle.

The effort required to raise the bells to a full circle ringing position.
A regular rhythm of the bells sounding the changes.

Starting teaching a beginner the art of bell control.
Feeling pleased when they become a member of the team.

The pride in winning a ringing competition.
A sense of achievement at the end of a peal or quarter peal.

Ringing for special occasions, such as weddings and funerals.
Ringing for the Platinum Jubilee of Queen Elizabeth in 2022.
Later for the passing of the Queen.
Ringing for the coronation of King Charles in May 2023.

At the end of a ringing session, the sound of silence that follows
the lowering down of the bells.

Numbers

Felicity Hydes

Misericord:
1. Ledge or `pity seat` to allow monks to rest in long services.
2. A small dagger to deliver a death stroke, to hasten the end.

Some unknowings dance with delight.
Yet, there is no intercourse, no dialogue
between Somebody and Nobody
in relief under the south aisle stalls.
Separated as they are by two skipping spies
and a cluster of mutant grapes;
you feel you are meant to laugh.

A commonplace book must have found
a journeyman`s hands, thin-skinned
and scarred; tongue-in-cheek.
Cribbed remorselessly from a vellum map –
sprawling geographies, unnavigated rivers,
camel trains and fuzzy edges.
A bunch of God mistakes in vegetable dyes;
this world square, that one flat.

And you, with your eyes between shoulder
blades, flicking lazy snakes that munch
on tails; you with your head perched only
on legs, just nose, forehead, chin and ears.
This mind likes to torment; this tyrant ridicules –
'sit, won`t you sit? Perch, take the weight off?'
Top heavy as you are, objectified –
the bestiary from which you came
unfit for any sort of modern incarnation.
You sway, unbalance, lean like a loon,
no waist, no rump, who needs a womb?
The drama of the `unpromised land`,
counting dots as you do in the `Great Game`.

And a silk road rises up in you, an ocean
of blue tiles, and from the clerestory,
your selfhood, your incompleteness;
the book of woman, never here to find.
But waxed, varnished, in need of constant polish,
our grotesques are what they always present –
gluttonous, covetous, envious curiosities.
Out of step, chasing after stolen fruit.

Noblesse Oblige

inspired by memorials in Ripon Cathedral

Maggie Cobbett

Commemorated in stained glass, Claude Eustace Ralph de Quincey Browne,
Shining example of his class, will be remembered by the town.

Yet what of Joe, the orphan boy, sent off by Lord and Lady Browne
As batman to their pride and joy when their whole world turned upside down?

They knew their own beloved Claude would much prefer to sketch and write.
Young Joe could shoulder every load, and workhouse boys knew how to fight.

No warrior he, their gentle son, yet fear of shame kept him at war
Until his trench was overrun, and he lay dying on the floor.

Joe, wounded too, still tended him. 'Rely on me, sir. You'll be fine.'
He waited till the stars grew dim and carried Claude back to the line.

Though in great pain and losing blood, Joe focused on his one intent:
To save his master from the mud before all energy was spent.

The surgeons did the best they could, but soon faint hope turned to despair.
Not every hurt can be withstood, and so it was with the young heir.

Without a word, he passed away, his loyal batman by his side.
Joe had no further part to play and, duty done, collapsed and died.

Prostrate with grief, the Brownes had Claude borne home by private ambulance,
Remains to be revered, adored. Brave Joe they left unmourned in France.

Commemorated in stained glass, Claude Eustace Ralph de Quincey Browne,
Shining example of his class, will be remembered by the town.

Tin Soldier

Kate Swann

You are not watching the traffic
alien vehicles   not from your time
you hold the hand of a pretty girl

her eyes on you in your uniform
your mind on this last day —
where will you fill your tin cup tomorrow

as you make your way
to the mud sodden trenches of war
her last touch of tenderness

breath of sweetness will come
to you in dreams on nights of fear
in days of fighting

for now you stand as one
captured in a cameo of stillness
traffic rushes by not watching you

Ripon

Timmy Anglais

Waiting for the bus feeling like a chump; it's almost
like they roll the dice to decide whether it's on
time, and when it does roll up late, I'm still
paying the same price.

The jobs are advertising, but they are only part time,
and when they're full time, I get told I'm not
right. I switched off the job search site like the
streetlights before midnight.

I could walk down the street and not see another soul
in months when it's cold.

A time warped reality clinging onto ancient charms.
Difference is met with open arms until it's too
different, then it's met with qualms.

Ignorance is coupled often with misunderstanding
and an unwillingness to change because it's been
longstanding.

With all this being said, you comfort me.

Bus to Ripon

Caroline Matusiak

on bus 36 sit down, pen steady
now pass village lanes, the field that floods
look, Ripley Cross is coming up already
then garden centre and busy pubs
on board there's always some conversation
of pets or home until someone leaves
with people heading to work or station
I sew and say, *Would you like one of these?*
and then I pack my bag with crochet hook
at the market place with trumpet loud
with writing pad and unread book
and step off right in the bustling crowd

but this is not a shopping trip today
inside my bag are words in ricochet

Going Downhill on a Bicycle

A lady's love song to a faithful friend

inspired by 'Going Down Hill On A Bicycle: A Boy's Song' by Henry Charles Beeching

Susan Perkins

We've seen our city's streets relaid,
patched and one-wayed,
widened and lined
with markings that fade.

I listen to your wheels' whirr, and there's a noise that
    sings
of mended rubber tyres, of spokes and oily chain,
of danger from a lorry or the cover of a drain.

You lean into the camber,
incline to left or right
see lights go red, green, amber
and wait with me for changes...

Who else knows the strangeness
of being part of a bike?

No longer fully human, chimera (or camera –
dark place, recording things?)
I too am tubes and cables, with inelastic springs.

Do you read the runes in rust?
Do you fear your end?
Oh, honestly I sometimes think

I'm going round the bend!

Malcom Dixon Man of Ripon

Terence Neal

Malcolm Dixon Man of Ripon
Clerk to the unwell
The bearer of errands for all and sundry
A friendly figure to all the folk he passed
On his way through the town he never left – his town
Except for national service in the RAF
A black and white photo in uniform of a dashing
    Brylcream Boy
Gallant as he was
His smile: his sword. His manners: his shield

Malcolm Dixon Man of Ripon
Fallen from that tree as a boy
And grew up into a man
Who never complained about his rearranged legs
The happy teeth – *alright Terry lad*
Three pints of the best – John Smith's – had to offer
Down the Black Swan on Sundays
With the merry men of the town
Before dinner

Malcolm Dixon Man of Ripon
Pictured in an old car straining up Sutton Bank, to
    Scarborough
The adopted kids on board
Fish and chips in Helmsley on the way back
Who spoke of the hereabouts as of a mythical land
Studley Pateley Brimham Sharow Wath
Who has earned the right to walk the town as a
    benign spirit
With that mile-wide smile for everyone along
    Blossomgate to feel
On his way to get the daily paper - there he goes

Malcolm Dixon Man of Ripon

Beneath the Bandstand

Nicky Hasson

They met beneath the bandstand, in the park,
As twilight blurred the vestiges of dark.
Two silver shadows locked in deep embrace,
Oblivious to time, event or place.

A lantern cast a frosted, spectral light,
That flickered in the welcoming of night.
The whispering of over-hanging trees,
Sweet murmurs, secret yearnings on the breeze.

She gazed at him and he gazed back at her,
Whilst all around became a faded blur.
That melted into blissful unaware,
As if only the two of them were there.

The creamy, soft translucence of her skin,
The palest azure gaze that drew him in.
She lured him deeper, kindling a fire,
Awash with desperate longing and desire.

The muted, pastel lilac of her dress,
Swirled low in softest drapes with each caress.
Warm fingers that entwined the balustrade,
The beating of their hearts a serenade.

Love inter-twined in ghostly silhouette,
As dusk immersed the starry-eyed duet.
Enveloped by the hazy evening mist,
They clasped each other tighter as they kissed.

The Ripon College Interview

Lesley Davy

To Ripon I came in 1972.
I was running so fast, I nearly lost a shoe!
The college looked lovely and very grand;
I clutched a blue box inside my hand.

The head of music was waiting for me.
It was him that I had come to see.
'Good morning,' he said with a very broad smile.
As he opened his diary and his big black file.

He asked, 'Is it percussion you want to play?'
T'was a glockenspiel that I had brought that day.
'Are you being serious?' is what he said.
'Oh yes,' I replied as I nodded my head.

'Okay,' he said, 'Play the piano for me now.'
With quivering hands and a very big frown.
I started to play, and music filled the room;
Some Mendelssohn calmed me down very soon.

A few weeks later a big envelope came,
I raced downstairs and saw it was my name.
The answer inside, I couldn't wait to know.
To Ripon college was I going to go?

A college place I had miraculously gained,
No longer in Liverpool would I remain.
I'd soon be part of the Ripon college team,
And I'd train to teach music; this was my dream!

Corridors of Learning

a tribute to life at Ripon College

Eileen Thompson

> Memory slips easily
> down polished corridors,
> where the raucous cry of
> 'Sheets!' each week sent students
> scrabbling to strip their beds.
>
> Corridors where we walked
> in shoes, boots and sandals,
> in slippers or bare feet,
> where we lingered to chat,
> where we scurried when late.
>
> Where Carole King's 'Tapestry'
> and Don Maclean's 'Vincent'
> drifted through open doors
> and settled in our minds,
> scoring permanent grooves.
>
> Where, fogged with free ouzo,
> we staggered to our beds,
> quads cramped from wild dancing,
> when the Athenians came
> to show us how to party.
>
> Where Reverend Ronnie marched
> with bagpipes, past the miles
> of noticeboards, spreading
> benevolent blessings on us
> poor hungover sinners.

Corridors where we ebbed and flowed,
surging in hormonal turmoil.
Where we rubbed off our rough edges,
polished our chosen paths, tumbling
out at last into our futures.

North Bridge

Carol Burdett Mayer

North Bridge - rising water
as the Ure widens
ducks paddle over fields

Fishing on the Ure

Kate Swann

The competition's on
fishermen stand   silent
by black chalk numbers
the river drags its heels
as each pair of eyes watch
for the giveaway flick of a tail

misted air fills with hatching Mayfly
sonorous clicks release
reels as thin slick gut
snakes languorously
over the weaving water
leaves no trail

each competitor weighs
the skill of their rivals
the confidence in every cast
until the silence is broken
by the slow beat of wings
a heron claims the prize

It Has to Lead to the Sea

Peter J Donnelly

I stand by the confluence
where the Skell meets the Ure
like a T-junction, reminding me
that you can't walk round a river
as I imagined you could
when I thought the word
was just another name for a lake.
Mrs Bradford read a story
about a wicked witch on one side
and a princess on the other,
and asked us how the witch
could catch the princess.
Mine was the only hand
that went up. *Wave her wand,*
cast a spell I could have said
but instead, she could walk round
the water. Being a witch
she could have walked on it
or made it disappear
but I never thought of that.
The teacher was kind and
smiling, said *Ah,* asked if a river
could be walked around.
This time all the other hands went up.
No Mrs Bradford agreed
before having to choose someone
to tell her why not, a reason
I have never forgotten.

The Limits

Felicity Hydes

Awake early,
as though condensation exhaled
by dawn needs permission
to quit the windows.

There is a special quality
to the silence; snow has fallen
since midnight, everything
is lost inside a sealed envelope.
You cannot work
this out for yourself.

Ahead on the path along the Skell,
the dog lingers, sniffing crushed
leaves, worrying to and fro.
Turns nothing over, not even
the expected frozen snail.

And a fence ahead, sometime a stile,
buckled and barbed:
`Private Land` - you have come
as far as you are able.
The black temptation is to mar
the untouched surface beyond.
Forked bird tracks must be special
messages skittering into
the undergrowth.
Mastered as you are, planet
of foggy breath and slip-sliding.

The Laver

Peter J Donnelly

The city's third river,
a tributary of a tributary.
Its name reminds me
of the French word to wash
yet it means a babbling brook.
It shares it with one in Snowdonia,
a name my aunt once gave
Ripon in a white winter.

Estonia was what she christened
the gravel at the shore
of the water where we played,
us little knowing then
there was a real place called that.
It's ripples failed to drown out
the noise we made, and the
barking of Badger the black labrador.

Birds of the Wetlands

Susanna Lewis

Dusk creeps in, gently at first
Orange to red as the sun says goodbye.
We wait patiently, not daring to breathe
Anxious, expectant, hopeful.
A faint pulse in the distance
Swarthy swirls fill the arctic winter air.
Endless ebony smoke trails
Delicate starlings join as one.
A wandering floating community
In harmony, together, in peace.
And then the dance of many
Becomes the dance of joyfulness.
As shadowy waves ebb and flow
Dip and soar across sunless skies.
A rare moment of perfect grace
Nature embraces beauty on every soar.
Heavenly stars emerge, show their light
Time to go, but just one more flight.
Wings tucked in, the reeds below
And starlings rest, the final show.

The Nature Reserve in Winter

a triversen

Sheila Whitfield

A frost-rimmed leaf
   and ice-edged pond
      mark the overnight freeze.

Pieces of branches lie on paths
   like abandoned staves after the recent battle
      with high winds.

Amongst a palette of faded colours,
   pale red bramble and yellowed rowan,
      raindrops jewel blackthorn twigs.

The contemporary contrast
   of a neon sunset
      flares against the ancient limestone cliffs.

Scored against the fading light
   a wavering arrowhead
      of homebound geese streams past.

The sky is ribbed in indigo
   as the day slowly dims
      to a robin's evening air.

Yet Another Autumn Poem

Sheila Whitfield

Into the reserve,
and feet turn towards favoured paths,
my mind already wandering.
Everything is still, somnolent, the wind
barely breathing through the trees,
only a blackbird chinking softly
in the undergrowth.
Then there it is,
a shock of tawny gold
patched into the green canopy.
The autumn spell has been cast.

Scientists helpfully inform us
that it's just to do with daylength
and chemicals, yet every year,
taken by surprise, we fall back
on our unknowing.

St John's, Sharow

Caroline Matusiak

'You have now reached your destination'

Graveyard, where our last page is written
inscribed, beside widow yew, lean headstones
bone grey, tear-wet with war's repetition.
These bookends, born and died, sculpted with crosses
defiantly indexing faces in time
but weathering still, with painful losses
as that airy transience, life, declines.

Inside church, stain glass heart flames red, blues flow,
as virgin fresh green grows new life, birthing
from between lead trace on a group below
glazed with the lull of friendly murmuring,
inviting the Spirit, colour again
our lives between the lines with rainbow pen.

Bishopton Woods

Leila Roberts

There's a time
Near the turn of the year,
The winter solstice,
When the fabric of the real, the normal, the how-things-are
Wears thin.
And – call it – a strangeness seems to
Seep through time's membrane.

The dog comes close
Walking at my knee
Ignoring rabbits
Looks up at me
Stays – uncharacteristically – near.

It's not silent, but seems so.
The river, flowing over rocks, is noisy.
A crow – noisy.

Why then does it seem so silent
In Bishopton woods, near the solstice
As if – something – is immanent?

Turning Leaves

Gemma Johnson

Autumn drapes the land in mist and gold,
Where shadows stretch, and daylight grows cold.
A hush lingers soft through the ancient trees,
Whispers of leaves in the evening breeze.
The deer move silently, shapes in the haze,
Ghostly and fleeting in twilight's maze.
Antlers rise through bracken and rust,
Wreathed in stillness, quiet as dusk.
Water lies still in the pond's embrace,
Mirroring skies as stars find their place.
Ruins stand dark against the dimming light,
Silent sentinels of encroaching night.
The forest bows to time's soft tread,
As day surrenders, sky burns red.
Footsteps fade where paths grow cold,
Nature's secrets in shadows unfold.
The season shifts with a quiet sigh,
Stars awaken as daylight dies.
Studley breathes as the darkness calls,
A world in balance as autumn falls.

Ghosts of Fountains Abbey

Susanna Lewis

Whispers of Yorkshire mist float gently
Weaving through cold stone ruins
Calling softly to ghostly monks
Who walk these Abbey halls

Hushed Latin words quietly spoken
Lingering in the empty nave
Prayers drift through cloister walls
Echoes of the past still sing

Unearthly shadows linger
Trembling in the smoky dust
As fading light sinks behind gritty rock
The Abbey stands tall, head held high

Spirits hover, rustling in the breeze
Candles flicker to pray and serve
But silence descends on this desolate place
A site of worship, no more

Grewelthorpe Gravediggers

Tim Harrison

In Shakespeare they are clowns,
their rough-cut wit
the set for our mortality.

But come with me;
through morning mists,
in country churchyard see
two lads dug deep in solemn work.
They dig for one they knew and loved;
not for him the vulgar comedy,
the mocking grin of JCB
dishonouring all
in soulless council cemetery,
but dignity
from honest toil with spade and sweat,
to celebrate his life,
to mourn his death.

Dusk Walk

Ian Clarke

Walking where the river runs silt slow,
redshank and tern share my silence.

Then past the old house,
with the path lost to long grass,

where I woke to a warm blue,
played until woodsmoke and harvest home.

In the roof beams now, the Milky Way,
birds chittering in the chimney of no one's address,

then back through the village,
as a breeze shakes free the last of the leaves,

to that familiar dropping dark at four,
disguised as something new.

Felling Larches

Tim Harrison

Phytophthora ramorum,
Sudden Larch Death by stealth gains ground,
takes us completely off guard,
locked down as we were,
hiding in fear from a different foe.

'Escape to the country!' the papers command.
Drafted we come,
come to Hackfall's follies and ferns,
to Nutwith's great larches;
from far and wide we come, from town, from city –
come in our thousands, media's conscripts,
yet each a refugee of sorts.

Carpe diem! Old Phytophthora,
(ever the chancer) seizes his moment, clinging to clart
on an army of wellies, trainers, high heels and boots
that (eschewing ankle-spraining, eroded tracks)
crash oblivious through the leafy growth

and then retreat –
drift slowly back,
back to half-forgotten jobs,
back to half-remembered lives:
discharged –
whilst hedgerows bloom
crumpled cans and cardboard coffee cups,
muddy trenches mock wildflower verges;
scars of insurgency remain.

But see! before all this,
see! Death already on his way,
blown by wind, driven by rain,
stalking larch, oak and chestnut,
sniping where he may.

See now! bald and wilted canopies,
branches bare and stark.
Look! gaping lesions, weeping sores:
fatal wounds on this dear bark.

O my larches! dying in this month
of fading light and falling leaf!
no cenotaph for you, no two minute silence,
but the steady wail of chainsaws-
the public voice of silent grief.

Staveley Starlings

Helen Watkinson

It starts imperceptibly
Small insect-like swarm catches the eye near dusk
Gathering pace to the reeds like blunt arrows
Birdbrain satnavs guiding in from all directions
To saturation point: then magically rising up
To throw dark shapes, twisting in the pink blue sky
An avian Mexican wave with the rushing sound
Of a thousand wings in unison
Then, performance over, refuge taken
In the darkening rushes

The Thornborough Henges

Paul Mills

From far off, coming on foot,
travellers make camp,
blue haze of wood-smoke over the river,
their gathering-place uphill where the land flattens.

Their dead buried here show us the sky:
cloud, wind,
so much light, skylarks.
I see one rise, vanish into its singing,
reappear or change into another.

In a wide surround of moors and dales
circles repeat the three aligned stars in Orion's belt,
on earth as it is elsewhere.

Not ten miles from my house, swifts are returning
from two million years to the same sky.

In six thousand, little has happened,
stones of Troy, Carthage, washed by the sea,
worn smooth as river-stones downstream
from the ruins of Fountains,
these circles still in their place, still open.

At home, after dark, when borders collapse,
I half-hear voices crossing through,
twig-snaps of approach; the stars, close.

Nidderdale

Sue Birch

A tapestry of fields drapes the valley ahead
Held together with a drystone wall thread
Bounded by hills and heather-clad moor
Nidderdale beckons you to go and explore

A sense of excitement – oh, where to go?
No matter the weather, sunshine or snow
Somewhere rugged with an incredible view
Or a quiet, leafy woodland, with visitors few

Footpaths criss-cross its meadows and moors
Giving insight into those who went before
For centuries, worked by a myriad of hands
Many thousands of feet have walked this land

The River Nidd at its heart, like an artery
Flowing calmly or like a raging sea
After storms and rainfall high up in the dale
Bring torrents of peaty water down the vale

An industrious landscape with ruins widespread
Like the ancient remains of mining lead
Land peppered with livestock, trees and barns
Pretty villages, chapels, follies and farms

Dams and reservoirs hide a life beneath
Old tracks and dwellings, now in water deep
Partially revealed in times of drought
But there's always lots of wildlife about

Strange-shaped rock formations glower and glare
Like The Druid's Writing Desk or Dancing Bear
And adventure awaits in deep gorges and gills
Where the curlew's cry echoes over the hills

Some say there's mightier dales north and west
But surely Nidderdale's up there with the best
Quieter and more off the beaten track
And as it's my 'local', I'm thankful for that

The Handkerchief Tree

in Harlow Carr Gardens

Claire Shackleton

The handkerchief tree is flowering today
Flowing over with freshly laundered white
Delicate draping blossoms that hang and gently sway

I remember fondly the Lady Kwan Yin and pray
For her bountiful compassion and for insight
The handkerchief tree is flowering today

Befriend the grief it's here to stay
She will catch your tears, lift them to the light
In delicate draping blossoms that hang and gently sway

Find the joy and the colour, in the every day
Enjoy the changing seasons and savour the sunlight
The handkerchief tree is flowering today

Ever chapter's end, heralds the dawn of a new day
Cultivate a holding presence, steady and upright
With delicate draping blossoms that hang and gently sway

Feel free to fall into her beautiful bouquet
To find your wings, let go take flight
The handkerchief tree is flowering today
With delicate draping blossoms that hang and gently sway

Swimming at Coffin Lake

Charlotte Wilson

As I drift, I am
Reminded of a picture –

Floating in prayerful repose,
Tethered by the petioles of lilies,
A maiden's milky curves,
Streaked with the congealed curd
Of blackened mud, lapped by
Silty liquid, smooth as satin,
Stroking, numb, her dappled skin –

Cold, cold as death.

As raindrop nipples bud
Upon the rippling membrane
Of the brooding, silent lake,
Dreaming eyes stare up at darkening skies –
This solemn scene shrouded
By curtains of lead-lined clouds.

The eponymous cists, side by side,
Gape, empty, on the shore –
A jumble of soft moss and rough-hewn
Angles – the nuns they once contained,
According to local lore, long decayed,
Their patient love, I assume, since consummated.

Oxygenated lungs feign weightlessness,
As friction's drag substitutes for
The land-locked tug of gravity, always
Clawing at mass with bony fingers.
I cling to the orange, plastic buoy
Tied, loosely, around my waist.

It is not too far to swim, but it is
Cool, cool as death
In the deep and circulating water,
Where the edges are warmer
And the ducks eye us warily in the weeds,
Awaiting our departure –

The shrill moment of emergence,
A shrieking burst of light and sound,
Grabbing for a solid hold and air –
As in another, golden time
Leaves drift slowly downwards,
Tangling in a corpse's hair.

Reverie Written in a Country Churchyard

Marilyn Longstaff

On a bench in Wycliffe Churchyard some unexpected sun
in this cold Spring – an undiscovered place so close to
where I live.

Our default picnic – sandwiches and a flask. The footpath
to the woods runs past us – occasional dog-walkers say
hello.

Blossom on the trees in the old vicarage garden, sundial
on the porch of the ancient stone church.

Here the air is thin – a sense of holiness, of something
other, a place that has stood through time – like us.

How many benches, how many picnics, once with kids,
now just us two – always in countryside, not always fine.

And all those churches, meeting houses, chapels, castles,
National Trust houses we took them to. Never asked them
if they wanted to go – they came.

And all those country walks and picnics in snow,
horizontal rain: soaking trousers and steady climbs – up
down, up – both of them now city kids (not kids anymore).

<u>Digression</u> so now I enter once again the secret old
familiar dread. Always the rose over the cess pit,
acknowledging I might have got things wrong.

This church and churchyard open to us all with the bonus
of a state-of-the-art lavatory. Not to be underestimated
after all those dry stone walls I've crouched behind.

Afternoon sunlight on ancient stone – honey coloured,
pitted with weathering: it looks warm and it warms to
the touch but it takes on the temperature of the season.

Slow to heat up, slow to cool down. And porous – not like
brick, the plaster inside the church bubbles with damp –
a constant battle.

An hour from now, we'll walk the river path along
the Tees, a path I've never walked before to Whorlton
Bridge (closed for repairs) and the fenced-off lido.

And we'll hear the echoes of all the families that came
for a day out, see the old shed that served ice creams,
when swimming in the river was what they did.

And they never knew it was wild.

Heartscape

Claire Shackleton

This body, these feet
Carry me, into the heartscape that lifts me
As I return again and again
To the beauty, and the bounty of the Lakeland hills

This body, these eyes
receiving the world
gift me the mountain vistas
the lie of the land
high mountain ridge traverses
long sharp edges
clefts in plateaus birthing watercourses
descending into winding silver ribbons
streams of serpentine curves sparkling
sun lit in the valley floor

This body, this feeling
alive in the landscape
Wide panoramic vistas
in a myriad shades of green
dappling the stone, the bones of the earth
Innumerable scree sides
scales on the backs of steeples and spires
Rising from chasms
That fall away
Into the mysterious deep

This body, this adventure
helps me find my courage
when invisibility cloaks the land
takes me into the unknown
engulfed by cloud, buffeted by wind
until the veil thins and the path reappears
and there are glimpses of crevasses and ridges
of smoothed sides and notched teeth edges
Of mountain tops and blue bodies of water
Rippling with wonder under big skies

In the mountains and valleys of life
This heartscape sustains me
Teaches me, inspires me, lives in me
As I journey on.

The Swing at Heptonstall

Paul Mills

Her mum pushes her on the playground swing
and her dad
keeps on pretending her two-year-old little feet
are knocking him over into the grass
so that she laughs, keeps on laughing
as he goes on clowning and falling about.

What line of chance, out of the untraceable,
brought them this *here*, this *now* among
the skylines and swallowed valleys?

White Bird

Peter Bell

White Bird
Against the blackness of the skerries
Bright amidst your dark companions
What is your secret?

You remind me of a high priestess of ancient legend,
        circled by your courtiers
Or a magic creature from a children's fairy tale

Alas, White Bird
Your time is short
Your doom foreshadowed
In your unique, uncanny glory

And in your tragic splendour
You speak to me
Of things I struggle to define
Of mysteries
Beyond the reach of narrative, or metaphor

White Bird
You speak to me
Of the transience—and resilience
Of Beauty

Salient

Philippa Graham

My grave is Salient,
In a place unknown.
Waiting for a ploughshare
To turn me over
Or a workman's shovel.
No honourable place
In a cemetery's neat rows
With the dignity of my name,
My rank and my fellows.

Now, on the last gate
Between home and Hades,
My name is confined forever
In a sandstone block,
Upon block, upon brick.
But, I am in the breath
That departs the evening's bugle cry
To those who cannot rest.

Fifty-four thousand souls;
Man, woman, child and beast.
Each name a brick to rebuild a town
From the rubble war wrought.

Whilst my spirit was freed
From the bloody trenches –
Those rat-runs towards death –
The cavernous craters
Swallowed me up
With mud and splinters
For five flesh-bought miles
Of freedom's land.
My blood and bones mix
With the soil as they rot,
Marked now only by a poppy's sway
That honours me day by day.

'*Ad Majorem Dei Gloriam*
They shall receive a crown of glory
That fadeth not away'

The Cosmonauts of Ulm

Andy Croft

> '*Der Mensch ist kein Vogel*'
> Brecht

When the Bishop told the waiting crowds
That the tailor was quite dead,
The crowd began to sing and dance with mirth;
'We knew he'd never fly,' they said,
'His head was in the clouds,
And now his pride has brought him down to earth.'

They left the tailor where he lay
Upon the broken stones,
So nobody would try to fly again;
His broken wings and broken bones
Reminders to obey
The heavy laws of gravity and men.

And so the world goes spinning by,
And upstart stars still fall,
Beneath our heavy boots the planet clings;
And only bird-brains still recall
How we once tried to fly
Around the broken earth on gorgeous wings.

Molyvos

Andy Croft

Our last day here, and though we don't intend it,
Already half the morning disappears
While we discuss how best we ought to spend it:
The Agora, perhaps, for souvenirs,
Or else the local sights – we could combine
The Turkish castle with the famous view,
The Roman dig, St Kiriaki's shrine,
The hot volcanic springs at Eftalou.
Instead, I'm sitting on this empty beach
And watching as you swim towards the shore,
Your graceful beauty always out of reach
Beyond my grasp. I could not love you more.
This sight I know will always stay with me,
Of you, love, running naked from the sea.

Mid-Atlantic

Leah Fletcher

In moving from the flat plains of Minnesota,
The land of Hiawatha and shopping malls,
To God's own rolling hills of Yorkshire,
Of Wuthering Heights and dry stone walls,

I left loved ones behind and something else:
Brash voices and vowels like wide open ranges,
Shamelessly sharing too much information,
And probing the lives of perfect strangers.

Because on the journey, a part of me sank,
Not like the permanently anchored Titanic,
But the bottom of its heavily floating iceberg,
Unmoored, submerged somewhere mid-Atlantic.

Deforestation

Molly Hall

The rainforest is a useless wasteland,
So don't tell me,
That it is exotic and bursting with precious lives,
Just imagine,
We could annihilate the rainforest in seconds,
It is simply untrue,
These rainforests are unique and irreplaceable,
Because,
You shouldn't care about these animals,
It's a lie to say,
We actually need the rainforests.

(Now read the poem backwards, line by line,
starting at the end.)

The Plates

Peter J Page

As through deep space our planet spins;
Tectonic plates inch on their way.
As man fights man and no one wins,
The mountains rise and then decay.
Beneath the crust the magmas warm
And fault lines strain and harbour stress,
All building up a coming storm
In which mankind could not count less.
Mankind – a feeble, foolish race
Which thinks itself the peer of gods,
But really ought to know its place
And own it knows the fearsome odds.
The Earth spins on; the future waits.
Our fate turns on tectonic plates.

The Movement of the People

Helen Watkinson

Since time began
Humans have explored
Seeking out new lands, territories
Discovering the next horizon
It seems built in the genes
To sail the sea, to satisfy
That wanderlust and curiosity
And strive for betterment
Until maybe finding a fertile place
To settle and call home.

But there are those who have to
Go: leave their own communities
Not of their own volition
Through famine, flood and fear
Not a move they'd planned to make
Hoping for humanity
And a haven; a sanctuary; a refuge
Somewhere to be still.

The Wishing Stone

John Ridley

Dropped from the heavens,
Like some half-sucked lozenge,
Embedded in the clearing, standing alone,
Its power enclosed in solid stone.
Who can doubt its strength?
Who can doubt its age and wisdom?
Cold to touch, strong and firm.
No child can pass without recognising
The place where dreams are made.
And standing on top with eyes tight shut,
The wishing begins …
Anything is possible, there are no limits …
But to tell would break the spell.

School Photograph (1957)

John Ridley

Standing still, silent in balanced rows,
Ribboned girls seated, hands on knees,
Their feet tucked neatly under benches.
Smiling boys standing, their heads full of schoolboy thoughts,
Of playground gangs and games and four-a-penny sweets.
Colourful thoughts in a grey world.
Bright smiles and faded half remembered tints;
Grey clothes against grey stone and frozen in time
On that March morning.
Was it such a grey world then?
We looked clean and well turned out in warm school clothes.
In short trousers and knitted woollies in the unfelt chill.
Glad to leave our lessons, doing our best to smile
And make the moment last, before going back inside.
Our teacher was not missing, but out of sight behind the lens;
Our eager pleasing smiles betrayed her.
Out of sight but still in control, and in response we did what she said,
And smiled … and smiled … and smiled.
Young eager eyes that once gazed into the camera lens
See a view of ourselves bright, smiling and new,
The way we used to be.

The Boy from My School Year Who's Doing Better Than Everyone Else

Nick Edwards

I sit alone, trousers round my ankles, rummaging
through Instagram.
Scroll, scroll, scr— stop.
I compose myself a moment, then puke across my
phone screen.
I cough, clear a filmy window with my thumb and
ogle, crestfallen.

The boy from my school year who's doing better
than everyone else is on holiday again. For the
second time in two years.
I zoom in on his girlfriend's face. Passable... very
passable.
Behind the happy couple, a Greek vista tumbles
smugly away from the restaurant veranda.

I open his profile. He grins. 407 followers, ugh.
'Leeds/London', his bio gloats. Make your mind
up, *Greg*. Save some cities for the rest of us, *Greg*.

I lock my phone and begin to wipe my bum.
I think about the time that Greg rugby tackled me so
hard that the Mr Barmby had to stroke my hair
until Dad arrived.
I flush.

The Waiting Tree

Molly Hall

An elaborate crowd of emerald-green, lush leaves
sing harmoniously in the powerful wind as though
calling to their unknown futures. Shining
brightly, the sun spreads joy and happiness to
its neighbours, the pristine, pure-white clouds and
the serene animals of the forest below.

The tree waits, and waits, year after year, watching
the busy world go by; the joyful parts
and the sad parts, and waits for something to happen
to itself. Everything changed except for that
tree until it looked up to the sapphire-blue
sky and realised she could touch the puffy
white clouds.

Realisation flooded through her as she thought
about how the tiny, feeble sapling had turned
into something remarkable.

Or So You Said One Day

Alexandre Mexis

Like Ulysses told his sailors
not to suffer from the sirens'charms
but still prefered to be tied
to the mast
of his vessel
I seem
tied to your love
be it with ropes
maybe made out
of your hair
or more likely
caught in your heresy
I try not to listen
to the echo
of your voice
your words
your spells
your delicacy
yet
after all this time
such a long odyssey
I am
but
still your prisoner
though
at least
I have a place to be
the chances
are
one day
I'll reach
my island again
hopefully
not like a wreck
nor

a ransomless reasonless pirate
but like the king
of my liberty

My Time Is Worth Less Now

Sadie Hasson

Puzzles, play-doh, dolls and duplo,
A morning playing with Mum
Early years childcare £4.10 an hour

Recipe books and sticky fingers
A cooling tray filled with scents of baking
In store baked goods 70p a loaf

Through the trees and over the river,
A leisurely stroll to playgroup
Petrol £1.36 a litre

Fruits hoarded like treasure
An autumn afternoon brambling
Jam 28p a jar

Play worn clothes
Another set darned and patched
New joggers £5 a pair

Shared joys
A childhood memory
My working mum guilt £11.44 an hour

Mum's Roast

Leah Fletcher

'What do you want for tea?' Mum said.
'I won't be home until May,' I said.
'You know how I like to prepare,' Mum said.
'May is three months away,' I said.

'What if beef goes on sale?' Mum said.
'Can't we play it by ear?' I said.
'You always liked my roast,' Mum said.
'Not for the past ten years,' I said.

'You're too old for my roast?' Mum said.
'I don't eat meat anymore,' I said.
'I'm sure that's just a phase,' Mum said.
'Going on ten years or more,' I said.

'What do you want instead?' Mum said.
'I *want* to discuss it in May,' I said.
'I just want to make you *happy*,' Mum said.
'Then let's get a takeaway,' I said.

Wounded silence. The air went dead.
'I'll get the beef, just in case,' Mum said.

La Mouette

Philippa Graham

I read a book today.
One I've read before
In a different life;
How does such a story change?
The words remain as they were:
A story of adventure
And romance,
Of pirates and soldiers,
Of cunning traps,
Of defiance.
Words that took me away with them.
The story does not change,
The roles are set.
The blackbird sings in the tree,
The heron poised, silent, in the pool
The seagull wheeling and diving
Fighting its own kind for
The fishermen's scraps.
And I, I have my role
Set by others but
The meaning has changed.
It is no longer the tale I read
In my youth.
I read anew of curlews and sanderlings,
Of a fish escaping the hook,
Of a nightjar tearing at the darkness.
I do not read of romance and adventure
But of a soul trapped,
A bird caged, a heron
Confined to the shallows,
The sanderling dependent on the mud
And the tide on its own ebb and flow.
It is the yearning for escape.
It is that tide that changes,
Running for its life to the sea

And I, the gull, I stretch my wings,
Look to the changing wind.
I hear its call and soar.
It is the seagull's story,
The lure of freedom.

Head Space

Nicky Hasson

Today I decided to spring-clean my brain,
Discard all the debris, start over again.
Expel all the fear and the hurt and the pain,
The shame and the blame and the downright mundane.

So I plugged in the hoover and twiddled the dial,
Set the suction control up to 'maximum pile'.
Switched it on at the mains, let it whirr for a while,
Then brandished the nozzle in resolute style.

Stuck the hose in my ear and allowed it to suck,
To extract all the crap and the rest of the muck.
Felt the fluff and the guff and the stuff come unstuck,
Inhibitions, suspicions and all of that yuck.

And I wiggled it slow and I wiggled it fast,
As my noggin vibrated in time to the blast.
And my skull was imploding, my eyes had gone glassed
As it purged me of everything grim from the past.

And the vacuum bag billowed and bulged with the weight,
As years of obstruction and decades of hate
Were sucked in the bag at spectacular rate,
And the more it inflated – the more I felt great!

Till suddenly, BANG! It exploded and burst;
My ears were ringing, but only at first.
As I peered through the smoke and was fearing the worst,
I saw all my nasties had widely dispersed.

Now I'm walking around with a smile on my face,
With nothing up top but a vast, empty space
Light-headed and giddy – a total nutcase,
All my worries, anxieties, gone without trace.

And oh, what a feeling! So liberal and free!
No negative thinking inhibiting me!
I can't help but think this is how it should be,
'Just empty your mind'… (that's a quote from Bruce Lee!).

Crystal Morning

Linda Birkinshaw

Shoulda put the washing out,
On that frosty autumn morning
When the sky was icy blue
And the grass was frozen white.
Shoulda got the washing out
On the line all spiky like barbed wire
And blackbirds were braving the cold
To pick the lingering berries.

Shoulda put the washing out,
Got the ice white sheets to dance
In the wintery sunlight.
When brave rays from the sun
Filtered through the toffee leaves of beaches
And sparkling droplets fell
Like glassy jewels
From the frosted branches of birches.

We thought it would last forever,
That crystal morning,
Sky as blue as a cornflower
And clear as cut glass.
When possibilities were endless.
We didn't see the clouds
Looming on the horizon,
Seeping like a shroud,
Spreading the darkness,
Hanging limply on our dreams.

The End of the Affair

Marilyn Longstaff

I loved ironing all our clothes, not socks of course,
or underwear. I'd separate the washing into piles,
his, then mine and finally the stuff we share. The joy
of steam, of making something smooth. The scent.
And when the kids were small it lasted hours,
a chance to disappear into my room, listen
to Sunday morning Archers' Omnibus
and Desert Island Discs.

Maybe this love affair started in my youth
provoked by my mother's useless ironing skills:
creases in collars, melting a hole in my nylon shirt.
She wasn't daft. As a young bride, she lovingly
pressed my father's best uniform trousers,
under a damp cloth, beautiful sharp creases
down the side seams. After that, of course,
he pressed his own.

Now I'm reduced to ironing a few flat things:
tea-towels, pillowcases, the odd tablecloth,
the rest enjoying the shame of 'rough dry'
as my mum would say, although in later years
she paid someone else to do it. Now, I can't
stand for long enough and I get too hot
and you can't sit down to iron can you?
But I can hear my dad, *If a job's worth doing*

it's worth doing well. Put your back into it.
Ah yes, and there's the rub.

When I Am Dead

Duncan Thompson

When I am dead and in my box
I'll leave you nothing but my socks
To pay you back for the all the stress
And all the sleepless nights and mess.

My comics won't be yours to read
No matter if you beg and plead
My DVDs I'll leave with glee
To my favourite charity.

My X-Box and all my favourite games
And all the paintings in their frames
Can all be given to my mates;
They can even have the dinner plates.

You might think this is just for fun
But I can promise you my son
I am not joking no, not me.
I'm being as serious as I can be.

I'll even give away my cash;
I know you think I'm being rash.
But you had better start to save
As you'll get nothing from my grave.

Boredom

Nick Edwards

The boffins at Nobel brought out a Prize for Boredom.
I had a fairly empty diary,
so signed up to have a go at reviving the lost art.
I stuffed my phone into my pocket and slumped
into the sofa.

So far so good.

A bloke with an interesting hat walked past the window.
I tutted.
This was going to prove harder than I thought.

The Waiting-Room Mirror

Peter Burgham

There's not much to be said in waiting-rooms.
Dead time sitting in unspoken queues,
Strangers walled silent behind newspaper clamour,
An old man grappling a coughing attack,
The clock ticking forward but time
Ticking back as you sift old magazines.
They don't put mirrors in waiting-rooms,
No glass reflection of yourself
Puffing and blowing,
Coming and going,
Awaiting announcements of age and health,
Heartache on pause until the journey resumes,
One-way to the same place, no change in between.
Love may not always be on time;
It may pass by on the other track,
The espresso's hiss mocking long-lost glamour.
Love may be just a headline from yesterday's news.
There's so much left unsaid in waiting-rooms.

For Real

Alexandre Mexis

For real
red leaves
leave
blood
on the streets
when Autumn
falls asleep
and drops my dreams
of green
with the rain
of my eyes

May

Leila Roberts

May is the mocking month
Counterfeiting winter with
Blizzards of blossoms

Pondlife

Charlotte Wilson

Weight is critical, and tension –
Feather-light, the skater propels on waves,
Buoyed by blind faith and captive air,
Striding across the algae-mottled trampoline
Like an adolescent, newly drunk on summer,
Trusting their bulk to divine cohesion
And the brave assumption
That nothing treacherous lurks beneath.

Sometimes I Don't Even Notice

Ben Stanbridge

Sometimes I don't even notice
The sway,
Of early morning summer corn,
Passing stories to fields beyond

Or that steeple,
In the distance,
Being a beacon of stability,
For generations gone

Those silent seconds,
When the unseen
Take a surprised rest
From their morning song

Or the rising sun behind me,
Lifting infinite shades of green,
For me
To bathe among.

Trekking

Peter Burgham

You may go
up a mountain
be guided
along well-trodden
paths / you may see
wondrous sights
and hear tales
of the mountain
you may marvel
at the guide's
knowledge &
wisdom
and return home
in the comforting glow
of the setting sun.

Or you may tread
where no path exists
claw your way
from crag to crag
and when you arrive
home
with cuts and bruises
you may know
so much more
about the mountain
and yourself.

The Poets

Timmy Anglais has lived in Ripon for over 20 years. His poem, 'Ripon', is about small city barriers. It is written from the perspective of a young person who is trying to navigate life.

Peter Bell was a tutor at Ripon College and has fond memories of the splendid campus, observing week by week the advance of spring, or the maturing of autumn. Since retiring he has spent his time exploring and writing about the wilds of Scotland. His book, *The Light Inaccessible: Reminiscences of a Wanderer in the Scottish Isles* (Zagava Press), assembles some of his thoughts about the Hebrides and Northern Isles of Scotland. His poem was inspired by an albino cormorant he witnessed last year in the remote Shiant Isles, which lie in the stormy seas of the Minch between Skye and Lewis.

Sue Birch, when younger, wrote poems at family gatherings in competition with her sister to see who could write the funniest poem. More recently, she has self-published two books of poetry for charity – one about the seasons where she lives, and another when she encouraged others to do so during COVID lockdown in 2020. Her poems appear in other publications, including the Ripon Poetry Festival anthology in 2023 and 2024. She enjoys writing about favourite places in Yorkshire and the natural world, but any topic is game!

Linda Birkinshaw's poetry can be sad and serious or gentle and light-hearted, with ideas triggered by nature and the seasons. She paints colour into them as on a canvas. She writes about dogs, because she loves them, and gets ideas when walking them in the lovely countryside that surrounds our city.

Peter Burgham is a York-based writer with 12 self-published collections of poetry. His debut collection, *Bird's Eye View*, was recommended as part of its quarterly review in autumn 2021 by *New Writing North*. He performs regularly at open mic events across Yorkshire, and is a member of Write-On Ripon! and North Yorkshire Stanza. As well as the traditional forms of poetry, he has published a series of photo-poems, centred on various locations such as York, Haxby and Liverpool. He has appeared in the last two editions of the Ripon Poetry Festival anthology.

Hazel Christelow's first poem was written at the age of eight thanks to an innate aptitude and a beautiful rural background. An exceptional teacher then furthered her knowledge of the great poets, past and present. Fast forward to later life in Ripon and the joy of grandchildren, three of whom sang in the cathedral choir. The history of this venerable pile, its iconic location, and its bells inspired her poem, 'The Bells'. Her wider poetic output includes an appreciation of Mediaeval manuscripts and abbey ruins, but also the quirky and humorous.

Ian Clarke had his first poem, celebrating the moon landing in 1969, published in a local paper when he was 15. His work is published widely in magazines, anthologies and online. His latest pamphlet, *Staying On* (Vole Books), was published in 2024 and launched at the Ripon Poetry Festival. He also contributed to *Celebrate* and *Creative Juices*, the fifth and sixth Ripon Poetry Festival anthologies.

Maggie Cobbett has lived in Ripon since 1986 and taught locally for many years. As a member of Ripon Writers' Group and Write-On Ripon!, she is a keen supporter of literary and other cultural events in our wonderful little city.

Andy Croft has written many books of poetry, including *Ghost Writer, Sticky, Three Men on the Metro* (with W.N. Herbert and Paul Summers), *Nineteen Forty-eight* (with Martin Rowson), *Les éléphants de Mudfog, Letters to Randall Swingler* and *The Sailors of Ulm*. Edited collections include *Red Sky at Night* (with Adrian Mitchell), *North by North East* (with Cynthia Fuller), *Not Just a Game* (with Sue Dymoke), *A Modern Don Juan* (with Nigel Thompson), *Speaking English* and *Smokestack Lightning*.

Lesley Davy started writing poems about her life a year ago. She came to study music and trained to be a teacher at Ripon College 1972-1975. Her interview was interesting; percussion was not treated as a serious instrument at that time. After she was observed playing timpani in York Minster, Ripon College employed a percussion teacher and bought some timpani. Also, she applied for a choral scholarship at Ripon Cathedral and was turned down as she was not male. She comes to Ripon when she can, especially to visit friends.

Peter J Donnelly lives in York where he works as a hospital secretary. He has family, including grandmother Hazel Christelow (also featured in this anthology), living in and around Ripon and regularly visits the area, which has been the inspiration behind many of his poems. He won second prize in the Ripon Poetry Festival competition in 2021 with a poem about the bus journey between York and Ripon, and has had poems included in the festival anthology for five years running. He is the author of two anthologies.

Nick Edwards is a comedy poet and proud cat uncle. He was born in Elgin, Scotland and moved to Copt Hewick near Ripon aged five. He spent his school life in Ripon, where he met many great people, including his partner of nine years, Lauren. They now live with their dog Pip near Wetherby, where he created and organises the Wetherby Festival Comedy Poem Competition.

Leah Fletcher, a transplant from the American Midwest, has lived in the Ripon area for over 15 years, grateful for its charms. She is a member of Write-On Ripon! and has participated in the Ripon Poetry Festival as author and editor.

Philippa Graham moved to Ripon with her family in the autumn of 2020, mid-pandemic. This was an easy and welcoming community to settle into. It was a time of new friendships and kindred spirits. In the last four years, she has become involved in several groups – far more than in pre-Ripon years – encompassing community groups, singing, history, and of course, writing. Both people and place have been an inspiration.

Molly Hall lives in Ripon and is in her second year at Ripon Grammar School. She has been writing poetry since she was 6 years old. Her poem, 'The Waiting Tree', is about growing up, inspired by a walk through nearby woods and trees' long lives compared to humans. It won first prize in the 12-18 years category of Ripon Poetry Festival 2024. Molly's poems have been published in every Ripon festival anthology for young people since 2017, and also earned prizes in 2019 and 2022. This year, she was also a judge for the under 11 category.

Tim Harrison is a poet and composer. His poems have featured in several publications by the Ripon Poetry Festival. As well as giving talks for the festival, a performance of his composition 'When Stars Fill Darkened Skies' with libretto by Andy Croft was the closing event in 2023. Tim lives in Grewelthorpe. Many of his poems reflect the sights and sounds of this small village just outside Ripon. 'Felling Larches' juxtaposes the human struggle with COVID and the struggle of the local woodlands with Larch Disease. 'Grewelthorpe Gravediggers' recounts an incident in the churchyard early one autumn morning.

Nicky Hasson is an enthusiastic poet who has lived in Ripon for 35 years and wouldn't want to live anywhere else! She specialises in light-hearted verse that is spiced with earthy undertones and a hefty splash of the ridiculous. She loves a blooming good laugh and a cheeky little merlot. She draws inspiration for her poems from people-watching and 'accidentally' overhearing other people's conversations. Nicky is a founder member of the Write-On Ripon! writing group and runs regular open mic events locally. She has had poems published in a range of anthologies and has a burning ambition to produce her own book…one day.

Sadie Hasson was born and bred a Yorkshire lass, but it's chance that brought her to Ripon. She and her husband found that they love the place and the people, so it was an easy decision to 'stay awhile amidst its ancient charms'. In fact, it's now the longest they've lived anywhere, and it's very much home to their family of two boys and a dog called Kevin. Ripon is the place where she has grown into her role as a mother, so she chose a poem that reflects on motherhood.

Felicity Hydes moved to Ripon 15 years ago, in the early stages of training as a Yorkshire woman, to take care of her parents, and now serves her fruitcake with cheese. As a guide at Ripon Cathedral, one poem reflects the impact of the glorious choir carvings on the observer. Her poem, 'The Limits', celebrates the spectacular countryside of the Ure and Skell valleys. All her poems are a journey from the inner voice to the outer physical transfiguration.

Gemma Johnson's entries are inspired by Ripon's rich heritage and natural beauty. 'Ripon's Heartbeat' captures the city's history and community. 'Turning Leaves' explores the autumnal landscape of Studley Royal, honouring Ripon's connection to nature and history. Together, these poems reflect the spirit of Ripon—where tradition, natural beauty, and a strong sense of community make it truly special.

Geoffrey W. Johnson has been involved in the team ringing the bells at Ripon Cathedral for the past 46 years, and has, along with the rest of the team, taught many people to ring over those years. He has also helped with ringing practices at West Tanfield, Masham, and Kirklington on many occasions. He especially enjoys to ring for weddings, Christmas services, and for the New Year celebrations, in addition to the Sunday morning services. He has also used a set of small handbells for tune ringing in local schools.

Susanna Lewis lives in Hampsthwaite, a village just south of Ripon. She is a regular visitor to Fountains Abbey and Ripon City Wetlands, the inspiration for her poems. History and the natural world play a big part in her life, which is why she is drawn to these two special locations. The atmosphere of the abbey never fails to inspire a short story or poem, and the story of the Cistercian monks who once lived at Fountains is fascinating. Ripon City Wetlands is well known for being the site of spectacular murmurations of starlings over the winter months and is a joy and privilege to witness.

Marilyn Longstaff lives in Darlington and is a member of Vane Women. In 2003, she received a Northern Promise Award from New Writing North and in 2005 gained her MA in Creative Writing from the University of Newcastle. Her third poetry book, *Raiment*, was selected by New Writing North's Read Regional in 2012. Her other books are: *Puritan Games, Sitting among the Hoppers, Articles of War* (2017) and *The Museum of Spare Parts* (2018). Her new collection, *Being Gemini,* was published by Smokestack Books in August 2024 and launched at the Ripon Poetry Festival in September.

Caroline Matusiak launched her first anthology, *The 36 from Ripon* (Radius), in 2024 at the Ripon Poetry Festival. Many of her sonnets and poems, inspired by the local area, were crafted on this bus. She was a winner in the 2023 Ripon Poetry Competition and presented her poems at the cathedral. Her poetry is written to be read aloud and she can be found at open mic nights. Now a member of the Festival Committee, she promotes poetry and local poets. She swims in sea and river.

Carol Burdett Mayer is originally from London, and has lived in the Ripon area since 1970. She began writing poetry by candlelight, in an old gamekeeper's cottage on the Norton Conyers Estate, surrounded by fields and wildlife. When connected to the National Grid a couple of months later, she was able to write more and to send off poems to small poetry press publications. She joined the British Haiku Society, and continues to have poems regularly published in their quarterly anthology, *Blithe Spirit*. A collection of her poems, *Rum Sauce*, came out in 2019. Carol is a member of Ripon Writers Group and contributes to Write-On Ripon.

Alexandre Mexis left the University College of Ripon and York Saint John thirty years ago after two years spent on the Ripon campus as an exchange student from France studying English literature. These two years changed his life forever, thanks to the people he met at college or in town – at the One Eyed Rat, for instance. He now teaches English literature at school and university in the south of France and has published four poetry collections.

Paul Mills has published several collections of poems, the most recent, *Nomad, f*rom Smokestack Books (2021). Others include *Voting for Spring,* from The Poetry Business (2010), which contains several poems about Ripon where he lives. One of his plays was performed at the West Yorkshire Playhouse in Leeds. A pamphlet collection, *You Should've Seen Us,* with film from the Yorkshire Film Archive, was shown at literature festivals in the North of England, including the Ripon Poetry Festival. His book on writing, *The Routledge Creative Writing Coursebook*, came out in 2006.

Terence Neal's poem is dedicated to his father-in-law, who sadly passed away 20 years ago. He remembers the grandfather to his three sons as a good and kind man – a man who loved Ripon and always welcomed people with the broadest smile. Terry currently lives in Thirsk after retiring as a primary school teacher. He taught for over 25 years – the last 20 years in Stokesley. He recently performed a poem at the open mic night at the Ripon Poetry Festival.

Peter Page has lived in Ripon since September 2012 and is currently Coordinator of Ripon Writers' Group (RWG), having joined the group shortly after moving to the city. His sonnet, 'The Plates', was drafted at an RWG Poetry Workshop held in Ripon and led by Andy Croft.

Susan Perkins has been an active member of Ripon Writers' Group for almost 20 years, reading at the Ripon Poetry Festival and having poems published in the associated anthologies. She belongs to a North Yorkshire farming family and writes about a life and people she knows, or has known. As a child, she read her mother's poetry books from her schooldays; 'Going Downhill on a Bicycle' echoes Henry Charles Beeching's, though his was subtitled 'A Boy's Song'. Hers is a tribute to a friend who rode her bike until the age of 80.

John Ridley trained as a teacher at Ripon College (1969-72) and taught in secondary and primary schools in North Yorkshire. He retired in 2009, after twenty-one years as a primary headteacher. Following his retirement, he taught Children's Literature at the Open University, until 2021. He now volunteers with the National Trust at Fountains Abbey.

Leila Roberts has lived in the Ripon area for over 35 years, first in Ripon itself and now in the nearby village of Mickley. One poem, 'Bishopton Woods', describes an experience in Ripon's Bishopton Woods one winter afternoon.

Claire Shackleton started writing poems as a child and continued – more off than on – since then. In 2023 she reconnected to her poetic self, and felt motivated to keep going. By chance she happened upon the 6th Ripon Poetry Festival, and gave her first ever public reading – of her poem 'The Glory' (a poem which changed her life) – at the open mic night. She was invited to join Write-On Ripon! and has been a regular participant since, volunteering at the festival in 2024. She has a soft spot for Ripon and was confirmed in the cathedral many years ago.

Ben Stanbridge is 29 years old, and lived in Ripon until he was 18. He recently moved back to Ripon after several years away. During that time, he discovered poetry, finding the precise nature of writing a very powerful tool to understand and integrate this in-between stage of his life. He is currently working on a personal anthology.

Kate Swann has lived in Ripon for the past 46 years, but her roots are in the Lake District. She spent her working life in the NHS, and since her retirement, has published one book of poetry and a biography. Her poetry reflects a love of rural life and its characters. Kate's poems have been published online, in anthologies and magazines. In 2019 Kate worked with a young composer to produce a song which was performed at the International Leeds Lieder Festival. She is currently working on a second book of poetry to be published in 2025.

Duncan Thompson studied teacher training at Ripon College from 1989 to 1993, and went on to teach and be headteacher in Barnsley and Wakefield. He retired in 2024 to concentrate on spreading the love of listening to and writing poetry through school visits. He has published two collections of poems for children, *Kamikaze Mouse* and *I Think My Cat Is Broken*. He regularly visits Ripon with his wife, who he met at Ripon college, and attends reunions.